Nephi and the Women

written by Tiffany Thomas
illustrated by Nikki Casassa

CFI • An imprint of Cedar Fort, Inc. • Springville, Utah

HARD WORDS:
Sariah, prophet, worried, women

PARENT TIP: If you or your child begin to feel frustrated about reading, take a break. Or stop and say a prayer.

This is Nephi.

Nephi is a
man of God.

This is Nephi's mom.
Her name is Sariah.

Sariah is
Lehi's wife.
She helps him.

5

Sariah believes Lehi is a prophet.

Sariah goes with Lehi
and lives in a tent.

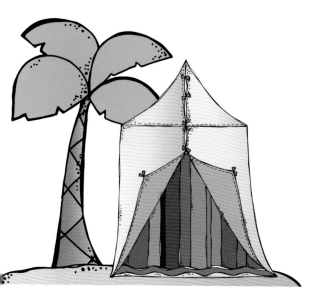

Nephi has a wife.
She goes, too.

At times Sariah feels
sad and worried.

But Sariah and the women
have faith in God.

Her family is safe.
She and the other
wives work hard.

Sariah and the
women are happy.

The end.

Text © 2022 Tiffany Thomas
Illustrations © 2022 Melonheadz Illustrating LLC

This is not an official publication of The Church of Jesus Christ of Latter-day Saints. The opinions and views expressed herein belong solely to the author and do not necessarily represent the opinions or views of Cedar Fort, Inc. Permission for the use of sources, graphics, and photos is also solely the responsibility of the author.

ISBN 13: 978-1-4621-4337-5

Published by CFI, an imprint of Cedar Fort, Inc. • 2373 W. 700 S., Suite 100, Springville, UT 84663
Distributed by Cedar Fort, Inc., www.cedarfort.com

Cover design and interior layout design by Shawnda T. Craig
Cover design © 2022 Cedar Fort, Inc.
Printed in China • Printed on acid-free paper
10 9 8 7 6 5 4 3 2 1